MAN & MUSIC

A survey of traditional non-European
musical instruments

by Jean Jenkins

Royal Scottish Museum 1983

ILLUSTRATION ACKNOWLEDGEMENTS
All illustrations are Crown copyright with the exception of:
The Trustees of The British Museum
91, 109
Professor Christoph von Fürer-Haimendorf
79, 82, 111, 118
Jean Jenkins
6, 8, 11, 12, 13, 15, 26, 29, 31, 32, 33, 34, 37, 45, 46, 47, 49, 52, 54,
56, 62, 63, 65, 66, 67, 69, 72, 74, 78, 84, 88, 90, 93, 101, 106, 121
The Metropolitan Museum of Art, New York
5
No illustration may be reproduced without written
permission.

© Crown Copyright
ISBN 0 900733 32 2

Photography by A L Hunter
Designed by HMSO Graphic Design, Edinburgh
Printed in Scotland for HMSO 6/83, D'd 8688851

NOTE
The numbers appearing in captions to the illustrations are
the registration numbers of objects in the collections of the
Royal Scottish Museum. Where such a number occurs in a
caption to a field photograph that particular instrument is in
the museum collections. The field photographs were taken
between 1965 and 1983.

Contents

Introduction   5
    Construction and Materials   7
    Performance   11
    Names   12

Stringed Instruments   13
    Musical Bows and Harps   14
    Lyres   19
    Lutes and Fiddles   21
    Zithers   37

Wind Instruments   42
    Flutes   43
    Reed Instruments   53
    Horns and Trumpets   60
    Bullroarers   65
    Mouth Harps   66

Rhythm Instruments   68
    Idiophones   69
    Drums   83

Selected Discology   92

Selected Bibliography   94

Introduction

This guide is intended for people who like to listen to music and who want to extend their knowledge of musical instruments to include those from Africa, Asia, Oceania and the Americas. The customary orchestral pattern of strings, wind and rhythm instruments is used here so that parallels can be seen between familiar European instruments and those perhaps less familiar from the rest of the world.

The majority of the musical instruments in this guide are in the collections of the Royal Scottish Museum. Because the appearance of unfamiliar instruments often puzzles those who cannot imagine how they might be played, wherever possible photographs of musicians with their instruments, rather than the instruments alone, form the illustrations. A discology has been included for those who would like to hear more non-European music. It should never be forgotten that musical instruments, however interesting to look at, have been made for a purpose–to produce music.

All over the world, and throughout history, music in some form has been an essential part of human life. Every linguistic, geographical or social grouping down to its smallest unit usually possesses several distinct musical traditions. As a result of specialist research over the past two or three decades, an increasing quantity of music from all continents is now available on records, radio and television, and yet this represents only a small proportion of the many musical traditions that exist. The music of a society expresses many facets of its culture: religion, history, myth, linguistic changes, marriage customs, birth and death ceremonies, economic values, agriculture, healing, games, humour. . . . There can be no single generally accepted classification system for such a mass of cultural material.

However, for musical instruments, although they range from the simple to the extremely complex, an agreed system of classification has been used by most authorities for half a century. This is based on acoustical principles, that is, the sound properties of the material from which the instrument is made, and the method of setting these into vibration. In the standard sequence of classification all instruments fall into one of four major groups:

1) idiophones (self-sounding instruments made of inherently resonant material, such as rattles)
2) membranophones (drums, where a stretched membrane is vibrated)
3) aerophones (wind instruments)
4) cordophones (stringed instruments)

In this book the sequence has been re-arranged to follow the more recognisable European pattern of strings, wind and rhythm.

Construction and Materials

Musical instruments can be very simple or highly complex in construction. Some objects, such as rattles made of dried seed pods, form instruments in their natural state. A length of bamboo makes a stamping tube; two equal-sized pieces of wood make a pair of clappers. A thin length of bamboo or a bird bone has its edge sharpened and finger-holes added to produce a flute. A flat piece of shaped wood has a hole bored for a cord and when twirled quickly gives the frightening sound of a bullroarer. A conch shell or an animal horn has a hole drilled in its side or end, making a trumpet. All these instruments and many more can easily be made by those who wish to play them.

Other instruments require specialist skills, and most stringed instruments and drums, as well as shawms, mouth organs and gongs, are made by craftsmen who are not necessarily musicians themselves. Drum makers, whether in Nepal or in West Africa, for example, carve the body of the drum, make the leather thongs for lacings, cure the skins for the drumheads, assemble the whole, and sell it to earn their living. All over the world the makers of instruments used in classical music are always professionals, and simpler traditional types are made by players. A shepherd boy can and usually does make his own flute, but the player of a classical Arabic lute will invariably purchase his 'ud from a specialist maker.

The animal, vegetable and mineral kingdoms all provide materials used in the construction of musical instruments. Obviously, in each area, whatever materials are most easily available will predominate–bamboo in the humid equatorial tropics, wood in the forested areas, conch shells for trumpets in the coastal regions, ivory horns where there are elephants, bronze gongs where metal and casting techniques exist, and discarded products of European origin such as pudding basins or tin cans for resonators, and petrol drums for the Trinidad 'steel drum' bands.

Vegetable matter is found in nearly all musical instruments, wood being the most useful: the bodies of lutes, for example, **11, 15**, and fiddles, for example, **25, 28**, harps **3, 5**, lyres **7, 9**, and zithers **43**, many drums **115, 116**, shawms **71**, whistles **55**, flutes **58**, and the bars of xylophones **93**, are all

7

made of wood. Sometimes an entire tree trunk may be hollowed-out to make a slit-drum **99**. At the other end of the scale, small pieces of wood are frequently found forming the bridges and tuning pegs of stringed instruments or tuning chocs for drums. Bamboo comes next in importance: split-stringed zithers **40**, stamping tubes **90**, mouth harps **88**, **89**, some slit-drums, clappers, flutes **46**, **47**, and pan-pipes **48**, *angklung* **103**, rasps, drums, mouth organs **75**, and trumpets **81**, may be made of bamboo. Other plants essential for some instruments include reeds for clarinets **65**, **66**, shawms **71**, and bagpipes **68**. Gourds (calabashes) form the resonators of a great many instruments: the harp-lute or *kora* **6** of the Mandingo people, the xylophones of West Africa **93**, the stick zither of Rajasthan in western India **37**, some *sansas* **107**, rattles **101**, and drums **114**, are a few of the instruments which depend upon gourds. Other vegetable matter used in instruments include seed pods and fruit and nut shells which are often used in dancing belts and anklets **102**; raffia and other plant fibres are used for thongs or strings **3**, while coconut shells act as the soundbox for many fiddles in Africa and South-east Asia **24**, **29**.

The animal kingdom also provides much material for musical instruments. Skin from goats, cattle, camels, sheep, snakes and even fish is a necessary part of all drums, and it is also widely used to cover the resonators of harps **3**, **4**, lyres **7**, **8**, lutes **1-14**, and fiddles **24-29**, to bind shawms **71**, as the wind reservoir of bagpipes **68**, **73**, as thongs for drums **121**, and the carrying straps of countless instruments. The internal organs of animals provide the gut strings used on the great majority of stringed instruments, although nylon strings are often used now, giving a very different timbre to the music. Horn and ivory are other common materials: with a hole bored in the side of a horn most African trumpets require no further work **84**, **85**, and horn is also used to provide the bell, or expanded lower portion, on many single reed instruments **68**. Bone too forms complete instruments. Bone flutes were made in neolithic times across northern Europe, as they are today in Central America. Tibetan pellet drums are made of human skullcaps **112**. Shells are also made into instruments: conch shell trumpets are used in most of Oceania **80**, but they may be found as far inland as the western desert of Rajasthan **78**, or in the Buddhist lamaist temples of Tibet, Mongolia and Nepal **79**. Tortoise shells sometimes form the body of a North African lute or a Sudanese lyre **8**, while an armadillo shell forms a guitar-shaped soundbox for the *charango* of Bolivia 22. Horsehair is another essential animal material. All fiddle bows require horsehair 24-35, and it is often twisted and used as the main string on fiddles in horse-breeding societies, such as those found in Mongolia, Kazakhastan and Ethiopia 28. Brightly-coloured feathers may decorate a rattle in South America or Hawaii, and an eagle's feather is used as a plectrum for the Algerian *kuitra* 15. Even such unlikely animal products as the thin membrane with which a spider protects her eggs is regularly used to give a buzzing sound to flutes and voice disguisers, and, especially in West Africa, to the resonators of xylophones 93.

Minerals also contribute substantially to the construction of musical instruments. Metals and a knowledge of metal-working techniques are important; so too are pottery and stone.

Some of the earliest known instruments are lithophones and stone chimes which formed the basis of much of the music of the Far East. 'Singing rocks' are also found in Nigeria, while a suspended slab of rock serves as a church bell in the mountains of Ethiopia. Stone is even carved into flutes by Canadian Indians who use argillite, a carboniferous shale 59. Pottery is more commonly used than stone. A thin pottery drum called a *darabuka* or *agoual* is used through-out the Arab world, and the two-toned double *naqqara* 120 is even more prevalent. Frame drums are sometimes made of pottery 114. Pottery is also used for whistles and bird calls, and for Pre-Columbian American whistling pots and globular flutes, which are often decorated with men and animals playing instruments as well as abstract designs 60. Metals are essential for much of the music in South-east Asia. The *gamelan* orchestras of Java 94 are composed of metallophones and gongs made of bronze, as are the bells and gongs of Burma, Tibet, China, Korea and Japan 95, 96. Cymbals may be of bronze or brass 92, and dancers' ankle bells are usually made of brass. The long trumpets of Tibet, Nepal, China and Burma 82, 83 may be copper, brass or bronze, while those used in processions throughout the Arab world from Central Asia to West Africa are generally of brass. Iron may occasionally be used for flutes, as in the Ivory Coast 62, and is very commonly found in mouth harps 89. Sympathetic strings (fine metal strings which lie below the principal strings and vibrate in sympathy) on an Indian *sarangi* are made of brass 33. Those of the 'foreign zither' or *yangching* of China are also of brass **42**. *Sansa* tongues are made of iron **107**. Some fiddle bows have metal bells on them **24, 29**. The pirouettes (lip rests) of shawms, the discs on the Japanese and the Ethiopian sistra **104**, the jingles on tambourines are all made of metal.

Finally, the cast-off products of European civilization, usually made of metal, often replace the original material. A sardine tin covered with skin takes the place of a wooden lute body; an aluminium pudding bowl makes the sound-box of a Ugandan lyre; old umbrella spokes are used for *sansa* tongues; a discarded wheel-drum replaces a gong in Morocco, and empty petrol drums make the exuberant steel bands of Trinidad. As fast as a product appears, human ingenuity fashions it into a musical instrument.

Performance

A few instruments are used solo: the shepherd plays his flute, a shaman his drum or his rattle, a fiddler sings the day's news, a praise singer chants to the tune of his *kora*.

Most instruments, however, are part of group activity. Not only did small ensembles exist, but large orchestras were part of ancient Egyptian culture, and of the Chinese and Western Asiatic courts. At least 3,000 years ago, large numbers of musicians were kept by several rulers, and there is written evidence that during the Han dynasty in China, about 2,000 years ago, the court maintained one orchestra to perform at religious ceremonies, one for archery at the palace, one for banquets and the harem, and a large military band. The total number of musicians was 829.

Thus the divisions between court, religious and military music were established early. We know only of the court music of the past: the classical or art systems of the Arabs, the Turks, the Persians, the Indians and the people of the Far East. (The terms 'classical', 'art' and 'court music' are often used interchangeably to refer to non-folk music.) Folk or traditional music was omitted from the formal lists because it was not performed by specialized musicians and was not considered sufficiently 'serene'. Traditional music has left little trace except in instruments.

Today, however, we know of African drum or xylophone ensembles, Indian castes of folk musicians, processional groups, village bands, itinerant musicians in South and Central America and in the desert regions of Africa and Asia. We know that the great traditions of classical music of the east continue, that the *gamelan* orchestras of Java and Bali are part of the daily life of the community. In short, music and musical instruments are alive and developing today, satisfying the needs of those who play and of those who listen, as they have done throughout history.

Names

Every regional and linguistic group has its own name for an instrument. In addition, there are often generic and specific names for many of them. A few names refer to only one instrument: for example, the Japanese board zither is a *koto*, the Arabic classical lute is an *'ud*, the West African harp-lute with twenty-one strings is a *kora*. Equally a name may refer to several different instruments. A *rebab* may be a spike fiddle with one string in Jordan, or with two strings in Bali; it may be a lute with a deep body and sympathetic strings in Afghanistan or a short fiddle, similar to that found on mediaeval European church sculpture, in Morocco; it may be a lyre in the Gulf States or in Ethiopia or in India; it may be long-necked fretted lute in Turkestan or the European-style viola played on the knee in Algeria. Moreover, the *rababa* of Ethiopia, which is played by Sudanese musicians, is called a *tanbur* in Sudan, but *tanbur* or *tambour* or *tambura* refers to dozens of different instruments. Unless an instrument has been collected in the area where it is played and the vernacular name used by the local musicians is recorded, ethnic musical instruments in museum collections can only have classification names or, perhaps, nineteenth century approximations of their actual names. This explains the variation of names in this book.

Stringed Instruments

Stringed instruments, or cordophones, have one or more strings held at tension, and the strings are made to sound by plucking, striking or by friction. The volume of sound is increased by the use of a resonator, usually, but not always, incorporated into the instrument.

Musical Bows and Harps

One of the simplest forms of stringed instrument is the musical bow, an arched piece of wood with its string stretched between two reeds. Sometimes the string is tapped with a stick, sometimes plucked with the fingers, sometimes rubbed with a stone, and the sound may be enhanced by placing it against a gourd, or in the player's mouth, or against a hollow tree. A cord dividing the string unequally will give two notes from the one bow.

To obtain more notes, several musical bows of differing lengths may be placed together on one resonator, giving a compound musical bow or pluriarc. Both simple musical bows and pluriarcs are found side by side in parts of Central Africa.

1 Pluriarc or multiple musical bow, Congo region, 1909.476.

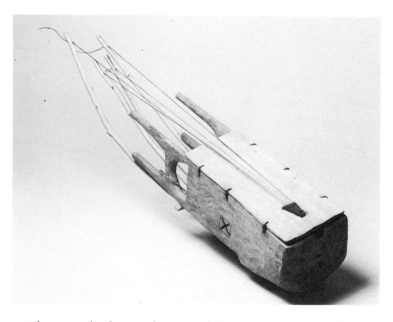

The simple form of musical bow is, or was until very recently, widely distributed. It was found in all continents, often used for religious purposes: to contact the spirits, to induce trance, to make rain, or to mourn the dead. Myths and legends about the musical bow abound, and these, together with its myriad uses and wide distribution, indicate great antiquity.

Harps, on the other hand, have a limited distribution, and almost all of them can be traced to the urban areas of the ancient world.

2 Musicians playing harp, lyre, lute and double flute. After an Egyptian tomb painting of about 1400 B.C. in the Metropolitan Museum of Art, New York.

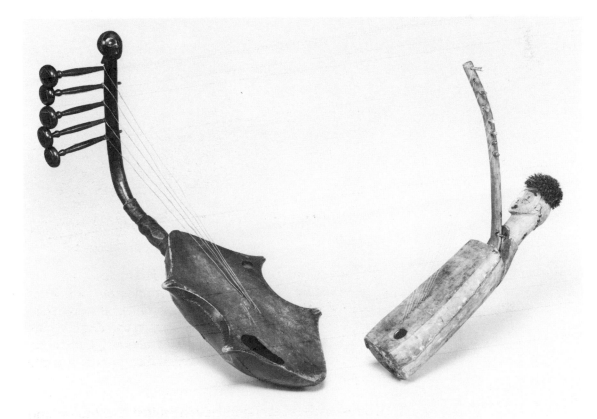

3 African harps with carved heads. Left: Azande people, southern Sudan, 1905.84. Right: Congo region, 1904.30. **15**

Harps have an arched or angled neck with a resonator permanently fixed to it: the strings are set into the resonator and run at an oblique angle to the neck where there is a tuning device such as rings or pegs. Harp strings are plucked. The complex construction of a harp indicates a high degree of musical specialisation, and it seems probable that in the ancient world, as indeed today in the areas where harps continue to be played, that a class or even a caste of musicians played harps and lyres. A characteristic of both harps and lyres is that each string is played open (that is, it gives only one note) and since the number of strings is necessarily limited, harps are almost invariably used, in Africa and Asia, to accompany song. An instrument so complicated as to require specialist makers tends also to be elaborately decorated, and African bow harps are often ornamented with carved heads, while Burmese bow harps are painted, gilded and ornamented with mica. Indian bow harps no longer exist, but the *wuj* of Nuristan in eastern Afghanistan is probably a descendant. It has also descended the social scale, and is now a peasant instrument, simple in construction and lacking decoration.

4 *Wuj,* bow harp, Nuristan, Afghanistan, 1980.255.

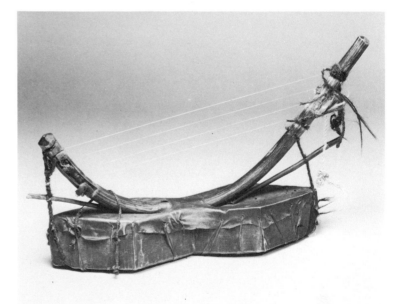

Angle harps have more strings than bow harps, but although they were popular court instruments and very frequently depicted in both Persian and Turkish miniatures of the sixteenth and seventeenth centuries, they no longer

5 Angle harp, played by a mounted musician. Detail from a 17th century Persian miniature painting.

exist in Asia. Various types of angle harps travelled south up the Nile many centuries ago and are still played in Central Africa.

An important West African instrument, played by Mandingo praise singers, those bards who sing the glories of the chief or the king, is the *kora*. This is a harp-lute: a lute because it has a body, in this case a large half-calabash covered with skin, and a neck; a harp because the long bridge does not lie on the face, but stands at a right-angle in the centre of the skin face, and both sides of the bridge are used to support the strings, which are then fastened to tuning rings along the long thin neck. Twenty-one strings are held at tension, and plucked with the fingers of both hands.

17

Kora players were formerly, and are in some cases even today, court musicians to kings or chiefs. They are professional musicians whose entire living is gained through playing music. In Guinea, Mali and Senegal, where most of them are found, they are called *griots*. They are often itinerant, singing the praises of political chiefs, the headmen of villages, and the patrons of city restaurants. *Griots* inherit from their fathers or uncles a huge repertoire of traditional music which remains even when they play high-life (West African popular dance music) in a night club for a living. They will return to their own villages regularly for important festivals. This renewal of the sources of their traditional music allows them to withstand the influence of incessant pop music on transistor radios.

6 *Kora,* harp-lute, played by a Manding musician, Ghana.

Lyres

Lyres consist of a body with two arms joined by a crossbar at the top. The body may be roughly rectangular (box lyres) or round (bowl lyres). The strings are attached to the base of the soundbox and fastened at the top with a tuning device, which is usually small sticks in the case of box lyres, or tuning rings of cotton or leather (or occasionally, nowadays, pegs) on bowl lyres.

Lyres share a common characteristic with harps: their strings are supported on a frame and played without fingering, so that each string gives only one note. From their pre-eminent position in the ancient world, harps and lyres have now become the least common of all the stringed instruments. We know of them from about 5,000 years ago in the great urban centres of Western Asia: there are three fine examples of the box lyre from the royal cemetery at Ur, in present-day Iraq, excavated by Sir Leonard Woolley.

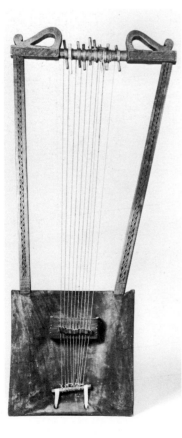

7 *Bagana,* box lyre with tuning sticks, Amhara people, central Ethiopia, 1980.382. A direct descendant of the 5,000 year old lyre found in the royal cemetery of Ur.

Two types of lyre existed side by side in the ancient world: box lyres with asymmetrical arms and heavy bodies decorated with silver and semi-precious stones, and bowl lyres with symmetrical arms, light in weight and easily carried. It would seem that box lyres were played by the urban nobility and bowl lyres by itinerant musicians. This seems to have been true not only in Sumeria, but also in ancient Egypt, Greece and Rome. The bowl lyre on the vase illustrated in Fig. 8 on the right is obviously light enough to have been carried easily in one hand. The same has been true of Ethiopia until the present day, where the bowl lyre was used for ballads, political songs and historical epics, and also played by itinerant musicians who sang of daily events in much the same fashion as was the case in ancient Greece. The box lyre was used by the nobility and educated priesthood, and reserved for the accompaniment of Christian religious allegories. Whereas the box lyre no longer exists today except in Ethiopia, the bowl lyre travelled south up the Nile much as harps did. They are, however, more frequently used, particularly as Sudanese slaves carried them to all parts of the Arabic world and even to such far-flung Muslim areas as Shiraz and India (where the Nizam of Hyderabad included them in his orchestra).

19

8 Bowl lyres, portable instruments with tuning rings, depicted on Greek vases of the 5th and 3rd centuries B.C. Left: 1872.23.10. Right: 1872.23.8.

9 *Kerar*, bowl lyre, Tigré people, Eritrea, Ethiopia.

Lutes and Fiddles

These instruments have a body and a neck; the strings are stretched from, or near, the base of the body to the end of the neck. Thus the vibrating length of the strings may be changed while playing by stopping with the fingers, either by pressing the string onto the neck or by touching it from the side. This differentiates them sharply from harps and lyres, where each note requires a separate string. Lutes may be either plucked or bowed; bowed lutes, where the strings are set in motion by the friction from a resined horsehair bow, are commonly called fiddles. These instruments comprise by far the greatest number of all stringed instruments, and the variety of lute forms is enormous.

Lutes arrived on the musical scene after their stringed predecessors, the harps and lyres, which were known by 3,000 B.C. and may have existed earlier. Lutes are first depicted on a few figurines and seals in Western Asia a thousand years later, and the earliest of those shown were light, portable instruments, possibly used by shepherds and nomadic tribesmen. They all had small bodies, very long necks and two strings which were plucked.

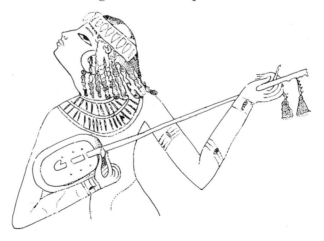

10 Musician playing a small pierced lute with leather tuning rings and thongs. After an Egyptian tomb painting of about 1400 B.C. in the Metropolitan Museum of Art, New York.

The vast proliferation of lutes began shortly after their first appearance. All Western Asia adopted the instrument which spread rapidly. It was simple to construct: a half-calabash, a piece of bamboo, or a hollowed-out wooden bowl acted as a soundbox, and the face was covered with skin; a hole was pierced to allow the long neck to come through the skin or the body itself. The strings were fixed to

21

the lower end of the neck and fastened at the far end with a tuning device, usually leather rings. Examples excavated in Egypt and Sumeria exist, but more important, we know from Egyptian tomb paintings **2**, **10** how they were played. Even more interesting is the fact that an almost identical instrument, the *kerouné*, is still used in the north of Sierra Leone **11**.

11 Fula musician playing a *kerouné,* a small pierced lute, northern Sierra Leone, 1980.213.

Its strings are fixed and also tuned in the same way as the ancient Egyptian lute. The *kerouné* has been the dominant lute of the area, and now that the much louder European guitars have been adopted, particularly by professional musicians, it might have been expected that the smaller 'old-fashioned' *kerouné* would soon disappear. Instead, the small pierced lute is an integral part of these modern musical groups and European guitars are tuned to the *kerouné* rather than the other way round **12**. Another development of the pierced lute is found in the Sahara, where the body of the lute becomes longer, the neck shorter, and a device for producing a buzzing sound, much enjoyed by Africans, is added. The *gurumi* player of Niger **13** is an itinerant musician; singing in Hausa he can cover a territory of

12 Group of itinerant musicians, Sierra Leone. The European guitars are tuned to the *kerouné*.

13 Hausa musician playing a *gurumi,* a pierced lute, Dosso, Niger, 1980.295.

23

hundreds of miles where that language is understood. Today, as thousands of years ago, the pierced lute, light and easy to carry, accompanies a travelling musician.

Long plucked lutes continue to be widely used in Asia also, although instead of having the neck pierce the body, it appears to grow from the body (even when in fact it is made separately and attached). Asian long lutes are usually made of wood, including the soundboard, and the necks are generally fretted, sometimes with moveable frets. Throughout the Asian steppes Kirghiz and Kazakh herdsmen play these two-stringed lutes. Long lutes with one or more additional strings are played in Turkey, Iraq, northern Afghanistan, Pakistan and India, Nepal and Tibet **14**, in Mongolia, China and Japan. Some are plucked with the fingers, or with a plectrum; some have gut strings and others metal; some are made of light wood, while others, such as the Japanese *shamisen*, can be extremely heavy. They vary considerably in size. Finally, there is an entire group of long lutes from the Indian sub-continent, with very wide necks and raised moveable frets, metal strings and often sympathetic strings as well. Best known of this group are the *sitar*, the Afghan *tambur* and the South Indian *vina*.

14 Tibetan musician playing a *dramyen,* a long barbed lute, Kathmandu Valley, Nepal, 1980.188.

These long lutes of Asia vary enormously in appearance, but even more so in use. They may accompany traditional music such as ballads or epics; they may act as solo instruments in art music in Turkey or China; some Sufi sects use them in religious music; they may constitute a string drone as in the Indian *tambura*, or give the basic rhythm to a group. They are also used in theatres and in film music. Long lutes, in fact, show more diversity of form and function than any other group of stringed instruments.

Short lutes are later arrivals on the musical scene. They are roughly pear-shaped, hollowed out of a single block of wood which tapers towards the upper end to make a neck/fingerboard. Short lutes are represented on figurines, friezes and frescoes from Central Asia of about 2,000 years ago. The spread of this new instrument was also rapid, but it is notable that unlike the long lutes with their multiplicity of uses, the short lutes tended to become the outstanding instrument of classical music. Perhaps the forms we know best are the Arabic ones, the *kuitra* of Algeria **15** and the *'ud* of all Arabia **16**. The pear-shaped body of the earliest lutes is most clearly seen in the *'ud* from North Yemen **23**. This form still exists in South-east Asia, where it was carried by Arab

15 Lute-maker playing his *kuitra* with an eagle-feather plectrum, Algiers, Algeria, 1980.273.

traders and called *gambus* or *kobuz*. It developed many different forms there and in the Far East. The Chinese *p'ip'a* **18** comes closest to the original pear-shaped lute, being almost identical in form with those represented on Turkestan frescoes of the sixth century. Like the Arabic *'ud* it is principally used in classical music. Both the *p'ip'a* and the

16 *'Ud,* the classical Arabic lute, Aleppo, Syria, 1980.314.

17 Short lute, Ainu people, Sakhalin Island, U.S.S.R., 1900.48.

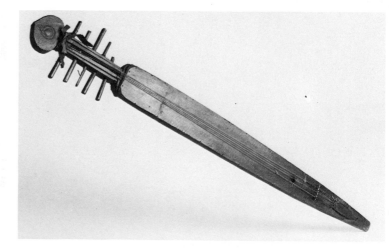

'ud require skilled craftsmanship on the part of the maker, and they are highly valued. Forms of short lutes can differ radically from the pear-shaped lute; the lute of the Ainu people of Japan **17**, and the *sapé* of Borneo **19**, or the *ketjapi* of Sulawesi (Celebes) **20**, give some idea of the variety.

18 *P'ip'a,* Chinese short lute, with shallow body and raised frets, 1911.232.32.

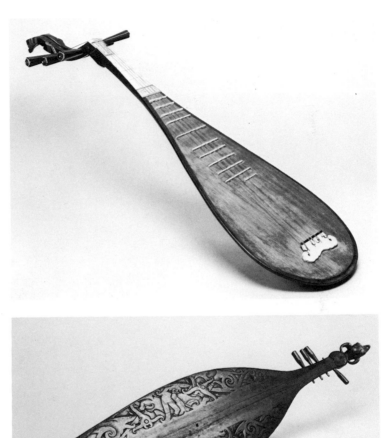

19 *Sapé,* short lute, Kalimantan (Borneo), 1981.133.

20 *Ketjapi,* short "boat lute", with high raised frets and metal strings, Sulawesi (Celebes), L.351.72.

Many European instruments evolved from short lutes. Among them was the guitar, first an instrument of classical music, and later adopted for traditional music, especially in Spain. From there it was taken to Central and South America. In some parts of the New World it became a large instrument played outdoors, and in others it became a small ensemble instrument, like the *charango* of Bolivia **22**. The deep-bodied lutes of the Indian sub-continent, such as the Afghan *rubab* and the Indian *rabab* **21**, add a new element to short lutes, namely sympathetic strings.

21 *Rabab,* deep-bodied short lute with sympathetic strings, north-west India, 1980.368.

22 *Charango,* Bolivia, 1906.493. A South American version of the Spanish guitar, using an armadillo shell for a soundbox.

23 '*Ud,* retaining the form of the earliest type of short lute, San 'a', North Yemen, 1980.330. This *'ud* folds to make it easier to transport.

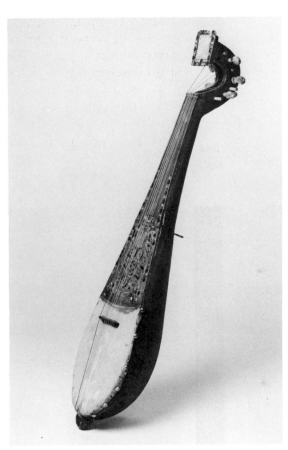

The technique of bowing–that is, causing the strings of a lute to sound by friction applied by an arched wooden board with a resined horsehair string–is relatively new in the history of stringed instruments. Bowing seems to have occurred in the Persian and Byzantine empires of the eighth and ninth centuries. During this dynamic period bows and bowing technique were transmitted to Islamic Africa and most of Asia. Very little change was needed to adopt the new idea apart from the introduction of higher and curved bridges. Thus pierced lutes became spike fiddles. They retain their long thin necks and small bodies, usually covered with skin. Since the bridge is higher the strings are normally lifted well above the neck. To change the vibrating length (that is, to change the note), the player touches the strings from the side, which means that in general only one string is used for melody, and the others may give a drone or an occasional chord. One-stringed fiddles such as the Ethiopian *masenqo* 28, the coconut-shell *pena* from Manipur in north-eastern India 24, the gourd *gogé* of Hausa musicians in Niger 26, and the Bedouin *rebab* of the deserts of Arabia are common. They are generally used by   29

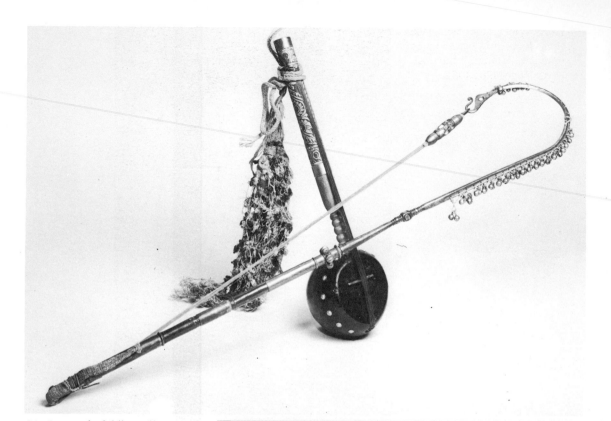

24 *Pena,* spike fiddle, and bow with pellet bells, Manipur, north-east India, 1872.31.2, A.

25 *Rebab,* spike fiddle, Kota Baharu, Malaysia, 1980.329,A.

26 *Gogé,* spike fiddle with one horse-hair string, played by an itinerant Hausa musician, Dosso, Niger, 1980.405,A.

28 *Masenqo,* spike fiddle with one horse-hair string, Ethiopia, 1980.381.

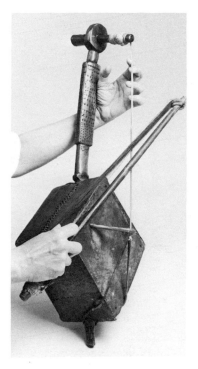

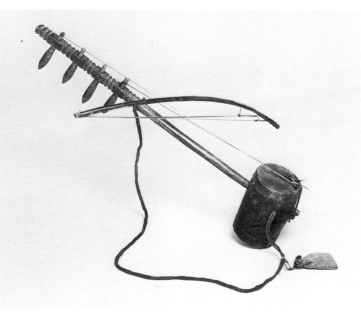

27 *Ho-xuur,* spike fiddle, Tibet, 1910.214,A. The bow is permanently fastened between the strings so that both pairs of strings are sounded simultaneously.

musicians who accompany themselves when singing poetry, genealogy, witty news in rhyme, and so on. A few of the spike fiddles have two or three strings, but these are most frequently used for other types of music. The Rajasthani *ravenhatta* accompanies the dancing priest who tells of the deeds of the god Pabuji **29**, and the *rabab* of Malaysia **25** and Indonesia is used to accompany and often to lead the *gamelan* orchestras of the courts and temples.

29 *Ravenhatta*, spike fiddle with sympathetic strings, Rajasthan, India, 1980.538,A.

Short lutes have also been adapted to the technique of bowing. Since their necks are broader and they have more and shorter strings, changing a note tends to be done by pressing the string against the neck. One example is the Black Sea fiddle, *kemençe karadeniz* **34**, which can also be seen on mediaeval European church carvings and paintings; another is the Moroccan classical *rebab*. The deep-bodied short lutes of the Indian sub-continent have also adopted the bow, and the variation in shapes is considerable. The Baluchi *saroz* **30** shows Central Asian origins with its waisted barbed body, which carries over to the Indian folk fiddle, the *sarinda*. The *kemayche* of the Rajasthani epic

30 *Saroz,* deep-bodied short fiddle, Baluchi people, south-west Pakistan, 1980.305,A.

31 Professional musicians playing a deep-bodied short fiddle called a *keymache,* a drum, *dholak,* and a shawm, *surunai,* Jaisalmer, India.

34   32 A bard accompanies his epic ballads on a *keymache*, Satto, Thar desert, Rajasthan, India.

33 Sindhi *sarangi,* a short deep-bodied fiddle with sympathetic strings, used by members of one caste of professional folk musicians, Rajasthan, India.

singers, however, has a deep circular body and a soundboard made of skin **32**. It is used not only by the bards, but in small ensembles of traditional musicians, where it fulfils a major role **31**. The sympathetic strings which are a feature of Indian lutes, such as the *rebab* and *sarod,* are also used in folk fiddles such as the Sindhi *sarangi,* where the tone of the bowed strings is considerably enriched by the thin metal strings threaded through small holes in the bridge, which vibrate when the gut strings above them are stroked with the bow **33**. Finally, a few bowed lutes arrived in the Americas, some from Siberia and some from Spain. The American Indians have adapted these to the materials available, as this fiddle from the Lengua Indians **35** demonstrates–although it must be remembered that while indigenous American Indian music was rich in idiophones, it had no stringed instruments.

35 A local version of the fiddle introduced by the Spaniards, Lengua Indians, Paraguay, 1930.519,A.

34 A small Black Sea fiddle, *kemençe karadeniz,* accompanies singing and dancing in Rize, north-eastern Turkey, 1980.324,A.

Zithers

Zithers have parallel strings stretched parallel to the entire length of the body. The soundbox may be a stick, a reed or a bamboo tube, a series of tubes forming a raft, a trough, or a board. Any of these soundboxes may act as the resonator, but a gourd may be added to increase the sound. Unlike the lutes and fiddles, they have no neck. They are most frequently plucked, but a few are struck.

The simplest form of zither is called a split-stringed instrument. Made of a length of bamboo, the strings are cut from the hard covering of the bamboo and are raised by small bridges at each end. Easy to make, the instrument has a very pleasant sound, either when tapped with light sticks or when plucked **40**. This type of instrument seems to have originated in South-east Asia, where bamboo is the most easily available material, and the simple split-stringed instrument is still played in Borneo, New Guinea, Malaysia, Bali and Sumatra. The instrument was brought by the Indonesians to Madagascar about a thousand years ago, and became so popular that the *valiha* is now regarded as the national instrument **40**. Sometimes small thin reeds are used in place of the bamboo, each one providing one string, and a series of these reeds may be bound together as in the Nigerian raft zither **39**. A zither can also be made of a scooped-out piece of wood, the narrow ends serving as bridges for the strings, which are strung continuously, some

36 Stick zither with raised frets and gourd resonator, Malawi, 1899.122.

37 *Jantar,* stick zither with raised frets and a gourd resonator at each end, Rajasthan, India, 1980.521.

38 Trough zithers. Top: northern Nigeria, 1949.142. Bottom: north-west Tanzania, 1981.26.

39 Split-stringed raft zither, Nigeria, 1953.123.

portions more tightly than others. These trough zithers are found in East and West Africa **38**, and generally accompany the recital of historical ballads, epics and genealogies.

The stick zither also originated in South-east Asia; in this instrument one or more gourds serve as soundboxes. The frets are high, sometimes carved from the stick itself as in this example from Malawi **36**, which came to East and Central Africa via Madagascar. More often the frets are made of another substance and fastened to the stick with a wax or rubber fixative. The *vina* is a very early Indian instrument. The form we know today dates from only about a thousand years ago, but the word *vina* was in use long before that and referred to a stringed instrument, possibly a harp. Stick zithers are carved on temples, and the goddess Saraswati is playing one on the eleventh century marble sculpture from Rajasthan **41.** The same instrument, but with raised frets, called a *jantar,* is used to this day in Rajasthan by the priests of the Bagrawat epic. Holding his *jantar* to him, the priest twirls as he sings the long history of the deity before a scroll painting depicting hundreds of scenes from the legend **37.**

41 *Vina,* stick zither with gourd resonators at each end, depicted on an 11th century sculpture, Rajasthan, India, 1956.576.

40 Split-stringed bamboo instruments. Top: Kalimantan (Borneo), 1909.358. Bottom: *valiha,* Madagascar, 1980.249.

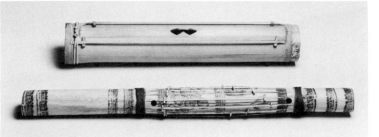

A plucked zither, used in classical Turkish and Arabic music, is the *kanun* (*qanun* in Arabic). This trapezoidal instrument has twenty-six triple gut strings, running over a soundboard of wood and skin; it uses metal keys, called ditals, to change the pitch. Plucked with small metal plectra on the fingers, the sound is delicate, the music complex **45.** The struck zither, on the other hand, has metal strings. Still 39 played in Iran, where light wooden beaters are used, and in Central Asia, the *santur* emigrated westwards across North Africa and eastwards into China (and from there to Japan and Korea). In China it is called *yang-ching* or 'foreign zither' **42**, to distinguish it from the long arched zither which has existed for at least three thousand years.

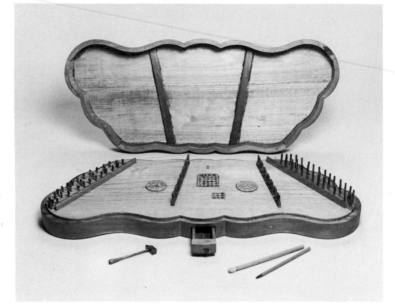

42 *Yang-ching* or "foreign zither", North China, 1905.145,A-E.

These long zithers belong exclusively to the Far East, having originated in China and spread from there to Japan, Korea, Vietnam and Mongolia. Although they vary in appearance and decoration, long zithers belong to two types, fretted and unfretted. All of them consist of a long narrow arched soundboard, the underside of which is closed by a flat board so that the whole instrument is the resonator. The strings are of twisted silk, which gives a clear yet delicate sound, and they are tuned to a pentatonic (five note) scale. The unfretted long zither was the instrument of Confucius, and it is still considered the instrument of philosophers, requiring great skill to play and a considerable knowledge to appreciate.

Fretted and unfretted long zithers are still played in China. As frequently happens in music, the instruments survive in their older forms in the countries to which they were exported. In this case, Japan and Korea have kept close to the originals. Two unfretted long zithers from Japan, the two-stringed *ni-gen-kin* and the seven-stringed *schichi-gen-kin* **43**, show the form and something of the variety of the unfretted long zither. The *koto* **43** today has fourteen

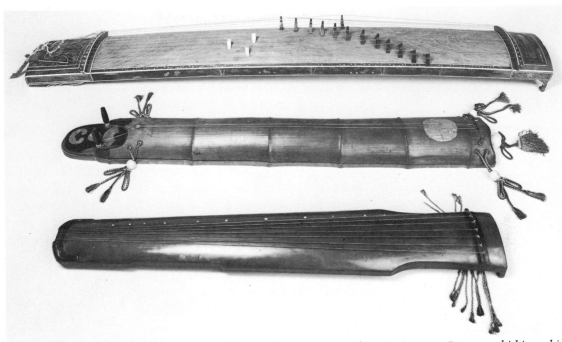

43 Japanese arched zithers. Top: *koto,* 1911.232.30,A-C. Centre: *ni-gen-kin,* 1911.232.26,A. Bottom: *schichi-gen-kin,* 1912.805.

45 *Kanun,* trapezoidal zither, Ankara, Turkey.

44 A 19th century Japanese wood block print of a courtesan playing the *koto,* 1887.745.44 (51).

twisted silk strings coated with wax, and a moveable bridge for each string; the player adds ivory (or plastic) nails to his own fingernails to produce a clearer tone. The *koto* is considered the greatest of Japanese classical instruments. A number of great musicians are honoured in Japan as virtuosi of the *koto* because of the skill required to master the playing techniques of different types of pressure, bridge movements and slides. A nineteenth century wood block print shows the playing method **44**.

41

Wind Instruments

Wind instruments or aerophones are those in, through or around which a quantity of air is made to vibrate. The air is enclosed in a cavity and may be set in motion by blowing against the sharpened edge of a pipe (flutes), by activating a free or beaten reed (reed instruments), or by the vibration of the player's lips (horns and trumpets). In a few instruments the outer air is made to vibrate by the whirling of a blade (bullroarers) or disc (spinning disc). The mouth harp depends on air in the oral cavity as well as its flexible tongue and is half aerophone, half idiophone.

Flutes

In playing a flute, the air is blown across the sharp edge of a mouth-hole. The length of the column of air, and therefore the pitch, is usually changed by means of fingerholes. The flute may be held vertically, obliquely or horizontally. While most are cylindrical in shape, a few are globular.

Flutes are found all over the world, in various forms. They are amongst the earliest-known instruments, having been found in ice deposits on palaeolithic sites in Siberia, neolithic bogs in Scandinavia, throughout the ancient world of Western Asia and the Mediterranean, in excavations in Africa, and in Central America. They are made of bone, wood, bamboo, stone, pottery and ivory. The forms vary as much as the materials of which they are made. Some have mouthpieces, as whistles do, while others use the end of the flute to blow across. Pan-pipes have different-sized pipes instead of fingerholes. Whistling pots are used half-filled with water. Some flutes are played in pairs, and in some areas the nostril, instead of the mouth, is the source of air.

Flutes can be classified according to how they are made: end-blown flutes, including pan-pipes; notched flutes; duct or whistle flutes, and cross (or transverse) flutes. Nose flutes may be of any of these types.

46 *Nay*, end-blown flute, Teheran, Iran, 1980.281.

End-blown flutes are the simplest of all to construct, being no more than a tube, usually bamboo, with the playing edge sharpened. This is still the preferred flute of the entire Islamic world. Called the *nay*, it is used in all classical music ensembles from North Africa through to Central Asia. However simple to make, the *nay* is difficult to play well **46**, for it is played with continuous breathing. In Turkey the refinement of a lip rest, usually made of horn, has been added **47**, and there the *nay* is used not only in classical music, but to aid the whirling dervishes of Konya. Other Sufi (religious brotherhood) groups in Algeria and Morocco use the *nay* to help induce trance and thus lead to direct contact with Allah.

47   *Nay*, Istanbul, Turkey, 1980.325. The Turkish *nay* has a lip-rest.

The other well-known type of end-blown flute is the pan-pipe. Pan-pipes comprise several different-sized lengths of pipe; there may be as few as three pipes or as many as fifty, varying in length from a few centimetres to almost a metre. Usually bonded together with raffia, they may also be glued. Pan-pipes may be in a single or a double row, and the tunings vary considerably. They were known to ancient

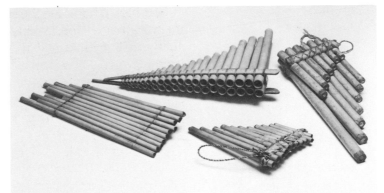

48 Bamboo pan-pipes. Clockwise from left: Tonga, 1956.1008 (collected by Captain Cook in 1778); Solomon Islands, 1902.192; Bolivia, 1906.490; Vanuatu (New Hebrides), 1889.566.

civilizations as far apart as China, Greece and Peru, and remain musically important in the Pacific **48**. Pan-pipes are also prevalent in many parts of Africa, as are dissociated pan-pipes—ensembles of people, each playing one end-blown flute giving a single note, and each adding his note at the correct moment. The Ghimira people of south-west Ethiopia had groups of players who achieved seemingly endless musical permutations and combinations.

49 Semai boy playing a nose flute, central Malay peninsula.

End-blown flutes are sometimes used as nose flutes, and this Semai boy from central Malaysia could play his flute either with his mouth or his nose, although he explained that it was easier with the latter **49**. Nose flutes, like panpipes, are most frequently found in the Pacific Islands **50**.

50 Oceanic nose flutes. Left to right: Fiji, 1868.79.6, 1904.130, 1895.304; Papua New Guinea, 1902.74; Maori people, New Zealand, U.C. 500.

Notched flutes, played almost vertically like the end-blown flutes, have a V-shaped or U-shaped sharpened notch cut into the top end of the flute to facilitate playing. They are found in Africa, and a great many one-note flute ensembles of eastern and southern Africa use notched, rather than end-blown, flutes. Notched flutes exist throughout South America. While the end-blown *nay* is an essential of music in the Islamic world, the notched flute has been prevalent in the art music of the Far East for about 3,000 years, and remains important to the present day. Notched flutes made of bamboo are kept from splitting by winding waxed thread around the pipe, or by using thicker bamboo **51**.

51 Japanese notched flutes of thick bamboo. Top to bottom: 1911.232.19, 1911.232.20, 1911.232.18.

A form of double-notched (also termed 'cupped embrochure') flute is common in Africa, where it is generally called a whistle or a cone flute. While they may be ensemble instruments, they are more frequently used in signalling, as here, in north-eastern Ivory Coast 52.

52 Lobi musician blowing a wooden whistle, north-east Ivory Coast.

While the notched flute is easier to play than the end-blown one, the simplest of all is the duct flute, where one blows into a mouth-hole which directs the stream of air to the sharpened edge of an opening cut into the tube. The easiest way to make such a mouthpiece is to cut a notch, and then tie a stiff piece of reed or raffia outside. Known as an

47

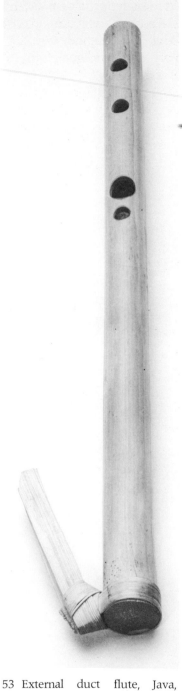

external duct flute or a ringed flageolet **53**, the *suling* is still played today in Java and particularly in Bali **54**, where ensembles of them are used in many *gamelan* orchestras. The more usual type of duct flute, however, has an internal mouthpiece. One of the most common duct flutes is the whistle. Often resembling the cone flute in appearance, central African whistles are somewhat more complex in construction: some blown from the end, some from the centre, some are tubular, others globular, some have two, three or four notes, some are made of wood, some of ivory, some are plain, others decorated **55**. Cylindrical duct flutes of the 'recorder' type, however, are by far the most common.

53 External duct flute, Java, 1980.223.

54 Two Balinese musicians each playing a *suling*, an external duct flute.

In the Islamic world, where the *nay* is used for art music, the duct flute belongs to love songs, dance music, shepherd's or village music **56**. The Batak tribes of Sumatra use this small flute **57**, together with a group of drums and gongs, to call the spirits. Indians of the Northwest Coast of Canada make stone duct flutes of argillite **59**. Finally, in Sind in eastern Pakistan and in Rajasthan, a pair of duct flutes called *algoza* or *satara* are played simultaneously by one musician, melody on one pipe, drone on the other **58**. A similar pair of flutes played by one musician can be seen in an Egyptian tomb painting of over 3,000 years ago **2**.

55 Whistles. Top: northern Nigeria, 1929.583. Bottom: Congo region, 1953.134-138.

56 *Kaval,* duct flute, Maçka, Turkey, 1980.257.

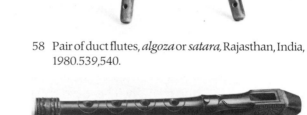

58 Pair of duct flutes, *algoza* or *satara,* Rajasthan, India, 1980.539,540.

59 Duct flute made of argillite, Haida Indians, Northwest Coast, Canada, 702.12.

57 Small duct flute, Karo Batak people, Sumatra, 1980.225.

60 Globular flutes. Far left: gourd, Papua New Guinea, 1980.356. Top left: pottery figurine, Pre-Columbian Peru, 1893.525. Below: pottery, Pre-Columbian Mexico, 1953.200. Right: six pigeon whistles, Peking, China, 1924.745-747, 1953.155-157.

Globular flutes are not common. However, the ancient Maya, Aztec and Inca civilizations of Pre-Columbian Central and South America produced a great number made of pottery, often in the shape of men or animals playing instruments **60**. Whistling pots are concentrated in Peru, where there seem to be as many forms as there are pots. In general, two inter-connecting pots are half-filled with water; the player blows into one, his breath forcing the water as well as the air into a compressed space and the air then comes through a whistle mouthpiece. This Peruvian example shows a man playing a flute. Globular flutes are found in other parts of the world, although never in such profusion. Afghanistan and the Indus Valley have pottery flutes, while a small gourd is used in New Guinea **60**, amongst the Maori, and in some other parts of Oceania. Perhaps the most unusual of these globular flutes is peculiar to nineteenth and early twentieth century Peking, where very light gourd and balsa wood whistles of differing sizes, to give different notes, are attached to the tail feathers of pigeons. The wind strikes the sharp edges and a flight of pigeons produces delicate notes as they circle and fly **60**.

Cross flutes, or transverse flutes, are side-blown and held horizontally. These are the great classical music flutes of the Far East. At least four different types, varying in size, may be distinguished in both China and Japan. Some are tightly bound between fingerholes with waxed thread, which is then lacquered to keep it in place **61**; others have a thin

61 *Bugaku fue,* transverse flute, Japan, 1911.232.21.

62 Iron transverse flute, made and played by a Senufo blacksmith, northern Ivory Coast.

membrane pasted over one hole to give a buzzing tone. The number of fingerholes may vary. In India, the god Krishna is always depicted playing the cross flute, especially in his role of shepherd charming the milkmaids with his celestial music. The same type of cross flute is used by farmers in the Kathmandu Valley, in the belief that its use is necessary to secure a good harvest **63**. Although not usually found in Africa, Senufo blacksmiths of the Ivory Coast make and play an iron cross flute which is credited with magical powers **62**. No cross flutes exist in the Americas.

63 Farmers playing the *baya* or transverse flute, Petan, Kathmandu Valley, Nepal, 1980.206.

Reed Instruments

In reed instruments the player's breath activates a thin vibrating reed which opens and closes rapidly, interrupting the flow of air through the tube. These include single beating reeds (usually called clarinets) and double beating reeds (shawms and oboes) as well as gourd pipes and bagpipes. A narrower reed set into a tube vibrates freely, and mouth organs belong to this group.

64 Idioglott clarinets. Top: Sumatra, 1980.237. Bottom: Türkmen, Afghanistan, 1980.259.

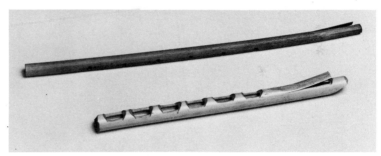

Single reed instruments may be simply a length of reed or cane in which an obliquely-cut tongue covers a small breath hole. Fingerholes can be cut in the cane lower down to make an idioglott clarinet, as small boys do in many areas. The player can always make an instrument; two such idioglott clarinets are shown, one from the Batak people of Sumatra and another from nomadic Türkmen in the north of Afghanistan 64. But this type of reed instrument has a major disadvantage: the reed is easily breakable and thus the whole instrument must be discarded. Therefore, one usually finds the tube with fingerholes carefully made, and an easily replaceable reed mouthpiece inserted into the top end. Single reed instruments are usually played in pairs which are attached to each other-the name 'double clarinet' is a term of convenience–and they are tuned a fraction of a note differently so that the beating will give a dynamic quality. Double clarinets are found all over the Islamic world: the *zumara* of Jordan 65 has two melody pipes, the Egyptian *arghul* has one melody pipe and a long, jointed drone. Often the wind reservoir is not the player's cheeks but a gourd, as in the Indian snake charmer's instrument 66, used also by the caste of professional folk musicians 67. Furthermore, the North African/Arabian bagpipes consist of a *zumara* used as a chanter with a small goatskin for a wind reservoir 68. The *tulum* or Turkish bagpipes from the Black Sea region 74 have a similar construction.

65 *Zumara,* a pair of single reed instruments fastened together, Petra, Jordan, 1980.287,A,B.

66 *Murli,* gourd pipes, Rajasthan, India, played with a friction drum by itinerant snake charmers.

67 *Murli,* Shiv, Rajasthan, India.

68 Single reed bagpipes, North
    Africa, 1947.120.

Double reed instruments may be either cylindrical, like the clarinets, or conical. Cylindrical ones are older, but are seldom used today. They have broad reeds, and their tone is more like that of a clarinet. The Kurds of Iran, Iraq and Turkey all play such an instrument to accompany ballads 69, which indicates that its tone is soft, while the Chinese *kwan* and the Japanese *hitchiriki* 70, whose name means the 'sad-toned tube', are used in classical music ensembles.

69 Man singing to the accompaniment of a *balaban,* a cylindrical reed instrument, Kurdistan, Iran, 1980.326,A,B.

The great majority of double reed instruments are conical in bore, for example, the shrill shawm of outdoor processional music which is used with drums and long trumpets over a very wide area from Morocco to Japan. Wherever the Arabs went, the shawm went with them. The *algaita* of Niger used in the court ensemble of the Sultan of Dosso 71, 72, the painted *surunai* of Malaysia, which is part of the shadow-puppet orchestra, and the elaborately-decorated *jyeling* of Tibetan lamaist temple music 71, are further examples of the raucous shawm with the pirouette as a lip rest. The chanter of most bagpipes also has a double reed (although the drone or drones have single reeds), and this simple type 73 is used from the Balkans to India–unless replaced by the elaborate and ubiquitous Scottish type of bagpipes.

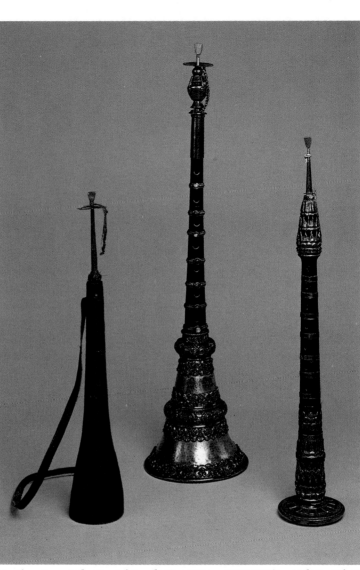

71 Shawms. Left to right: *algaita,* Niger, 1980.403,A; *jyeling,* Tibet, 1910.215,A; *surunai,* Malaysia, 1980.327,A.

70 *Hitchiriki,* a cylindrical double reed instrument, Japan, 1911.232.22.

72 The *algaita,* or shawm, is the melody instrument of the Sultan of Dosso's "band", Niger, 1980.405.

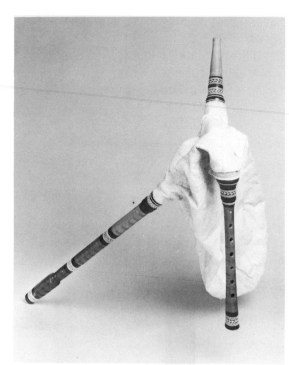

73 *Gayda,* bagpipes with a double reed in the chanter and a single reed in the drone, Rodopi mountains, Bulgaria, 1980.275.

74 Shepherd playing the *tulum,* bagpipes with single reeds, Rize, north-east Turkey.

75 Mouth organs. Left to right: set of five free reed instruments or "dissociated mouth organ", Thailand, 1980.316-320; mouth organ, Sarawak (Borneo), 1894.103; *shô,* the mouth organ used in classical music, Japan, 1911.232.2.

76 Lacquer bowl showing a mouth organ being played during a dance, Burma, 1960.402.

Free reed instruments have a sound as soft as that of the shawm is shrill. The narrow reed is cut into or inserted into a tube and can move backwards and forwards freely when the air in the tube vibrates. Each tube gives only one note, and they are occasionally used in an ensemble as in northern Thailand **75**. Usually, however, they are made into mouth organs (that is, several pipes of different lengths are set into a wind chest and several notes can be played at the same time). Originating in South-east Asia, mouth organs are still used in Borneo by the Dyaks **75**, and by the hill tribes of northern Thailand **77**, and Laos. They also form part of the classical music ensembles of Japan **75**, China and Korea, and are used in the art music of Burma **76**. The sound of the mouth organ is delicate and ethereal, which explains why, in many areas, men use it to accompany courting songs.

77 Mouth organ played by Miao performer, north-east Thailand.

Horns and Trumpets

In horns and trumpets the compressed lips of the player act as the reed, and no mouthpiece except a hole is needed, although it may occur. Horns are usually curved, with a conical bore, while trumpets are straight with a cylindrical bore; but in traditional instruments the terms tend to be used interchangeably, since these distinctions are difficult to make. Animal horns and conch shells require only that a mouth-hole be bored in the side or the end. Rajasthan musicians, as most Indians, blow them from the end **78**, as do the Tibetans and the Sherpas of northern Nepal, for whom it is a required instrument in the Buddhist temple ritual **79, 80**. End-blown, it is also used by Maoris, Fijians and Japanese **80**, but on many Pacific islands the mouth-hole is at the side. Animal horns tend to be blown from the side. Throughout Africa, one finds ivory horns as well as rams' and antelopes' horns, all side-blown. Benin bronzes depict this side-blown horn, and many tribes in West Africa, like the

78 Conch shell trumpet, Jodhpur, India.

79 Conch shell trumpets used in lamaist Buddhist temple ceremonies, Sherpa people, northern Nepal.

80 End-blown conch shell trumpets. Left to right: Maori people, New Zealand, 1951.377; Fiji, 1924.803; Nepal, 1980.209; Japan, 1911.232.11.

Guro of the Ivory Coast, have horn ensembles 84, using side-blown horns. Some groups in Zaire use very long end-blown ivory horns; the sound of such an ensemble is startlingly deep and powerful. One can form an idea of the decoration with which ivory horns may be embellished from these five examples 85. It may be noted that it is rare to find a musical instrument, however humble, which is totally undecorated. Straight trumpets are sometimes made of wood or of bamboo, as in New Guinea 81, but are much more frequently made of metal and provided with a mouthpiece. These are found throughout the Islamic world, where they are used with the shawm and drum for processional music, and by the court musicians of sultans and emirs, as well as to signal the time of the religious fasting month of Ramadan, and to lead armies into war. Turkish, Persian and Moghul miniatures show trumpeters accompanying armies into

81 Bamboo trumpet, Asmat people, Irian Jaya, Indonesia, 1970.964.

82 Telescopic trumpets, used in lamaist Buddhist religious ceremonies, Sherpa people, northern Nepal.

83 Bronze trumpet with two fishes' heads for bells, Burma, 1968.686.

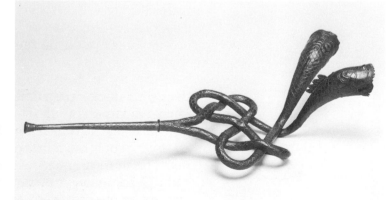

84 Ivory side-blown trumpet, Guro people, Ivory Coast.

85 African side-blown ivory trumpets. Top to bottom: southern Nigeria, 1911.189; Azande people, southern Sudan, 1906.565; Egypt, 1930.726; Masai people, Kenya, 1928.197; Congo, 1902.309.

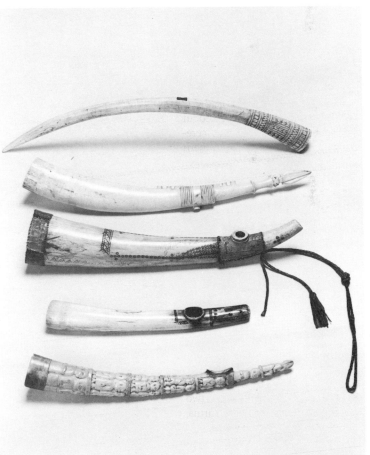

battle. The longer the trumpet the deeper the sound, and the telescopic trumpets of Tibet and Nepal are often over two metres in length when extended **82**. Occasionally one finds a double bell on a trumpet, as in this dragon-headed example from Burma **83**, or in the straight trumpets from the Sahara. These long trumpets are often played with the bell resting on the ground or on the shoulders of small boys.

63

One very special long trumpet, end-blown, is the *didgeridoo* used by the Australian Aborigines of North-east Arnhem Land. A branch of a tree, preferably hollowed-out by termites, is selected for its length–which may be nearly two metres–and straight appearance. Elaborately incised and coloured with earth pigments, this is a combined trumpet and voice disguiser **86**, whose rhythmic droning sound, in conjunction with the buzzing and roaring of the bullroarer, is part of the ritual and magic ceremonial of these desert-dwellers.

86 Didjeridus, Australian Aborigines, Arnhem Land, 1981.438-439.

Bullroarers

Bullroarers belong to that special group of wind instruments which create vibration in the outer air by whirling a flat wooden or bone blade on a string. Bone bullroarers have been found on palaeolithic sites. The instrument is still used in South America, in parts of Africa, Asia and the Pacific, but especially by the Australian Aborigines **87**. Its roaring noise is almost invariably associated with religion and magic, with the voices of spirits, of gods, of ancestors, and of demons. The faster it whirls, the higher the pitch, and the shaman or priest wielding the bullroarer is the powerful medium through whom the supernatural powers act.

87 Australian Aborigine bullroarers, with cords of human hair. Top: 1909.532.6. Bottom: 1909.532.7.

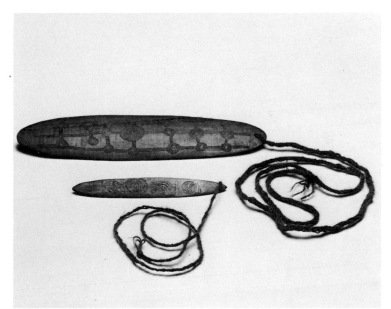

Mouth Harps

These small instruments consist of a frame of bamboo or iron and a flexible tongue which is made to vibrate by plucking it with the finger or by pulling on a cord. The frame is held against the teeth. The reason for including it in aerophones is that the mouth cavity and the air in it act as a resonator and amplify the harmonics. Thus it is the position

88 Bamboo mouth harp, the tongue vibrated by pulling a cord, Toba Batak people, Sumatra, 1980.231,A.

of the player's lips, tongue and cheeks at any given moment which determines the pitch and therefore the melody. Commonly called 'jew's harps', and arguably 'jaw's harps', they are here described as mouth harps.

Bamboo mouth harps are found in Oceania, throughout Indonesia 89, and in many parts of Asia. They are frequently plucked with a cord which may be attached to a clapper to accentuate the rhythm, as among the Toba Bataks of Sumatra 88, 89, or to an additional bamboo resonator, as in Bali 89, where they also use very small examples called *gengongs* to imitate the sound of a chorus of frogs. In Mongolia they not only play the bamboo mouth harp, but imitate the sound to make 'mouth music' when they do not have the instrument. In some areas such as Central Asia and India, bamboo and iron mouth harps are found side by side. The bamboo instrument in particular is used for courting and for love songs, and there are parts of the Indian sub-continent where its music is considered so seductive that its use is forbidden during planting and harvest time, when people cannot be spared from their work. The iron mouth harp is less intimate, being louder and clearer. In Afghanistan, Baluchistan and Rajasthan it is called the *chang*, which was the name of the Persian and Arabic angle harp, a complex stringed instrument which also had a delicate tone. Although mouth harps are generally used for love songs, small folk ensembles in Baluchistan and in northern Afghanistan have recently used it as a rhythm instrument, to replace the drum in accompanying two or three stringed instruments.

89 Mouth harps. Clockwise from left: small iron mouth harp, north-east Afghanistan, 1980.265; iron mouth harp, Rajasthan, India, 1980.331; bamboo mouth harp with case, Karo Batak people, Sumatra, 1980.229,A; bamboo mouth harp with resonator/case, Bali, 1980.239,A; bamboo mouth harp, Papua New Guinea, 1898.427; bamboo mouth harp with clapper, Toba Batak people, Sumatra, 1980.231,A; bamboo mouth harp, Karo Batak people, Sumatra, 1980.230.

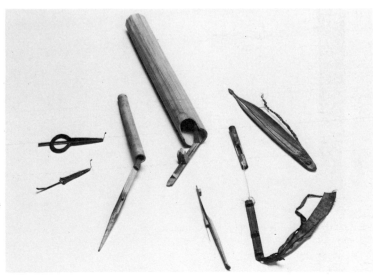

Rhythm Instruments

The great range of instruments which provide rhythm to music all over the world divides into two major groups. One group consists of instruments made of inherently resonant materials, most but not all of which are sounded by striking, that is, percussion. A few are resonated by plucking flexible material or by friction. Because it is the material itself which is vibrated, rather than a string or column of air or a stretched membrane, these are called self-sounding instruments or idiophones. The other group comprises drums, or membranophones, in which skin is stretched over a body and beaten to make it vibrate.

Idiophones

Percussion idiophones form a series of groups of instruments, some simple, some complex in construction. Clappers are two similar objects which are struck together, and while these may be simply two pieces of wood, the hardness or density of the wood as well as its size and shape influences the sound. Concussion sticks are used in most parts of the world: they are the earliest known Egyptian instruments, although the ones of either wood or ivory, shaped like a pair of hands **92**, are a later development. The Japanese woodblocks are thick **92**, while those of Chinese rosewood are thinner, and three are often used instead of two. In Turkey they are of thin dark wood, used in the manner of castanets **91**, or wooden spoons, often played as a virtuoso instrument **92**. Another widespread type is made of metal, namely the cymbals, large or small, of the Islamic world and the countries of the Far East. They may be tiny, or like those used in lamaist worship, large and of bronze **92**. Their form may permit them to be clashed together **92**, or beaten with a metal rod.

A second group of struck idiophones is even simpler and consists merely of logs, troughs, boards, or wooden or leather shields. These are stamped idiophones, which are pounded against the ground or against a piece of wood or bamboo. In central Malaysia the bamboos are tuned and accompany songs asking for a good harvest or for rain **90**.

91 Girl playing clappers, 17th century Turkish miniature painting (reproduced with the permission of the Trustees of the British Museum).

90 Bamboo stamping tubes, Semai people, central Malay peninsula.

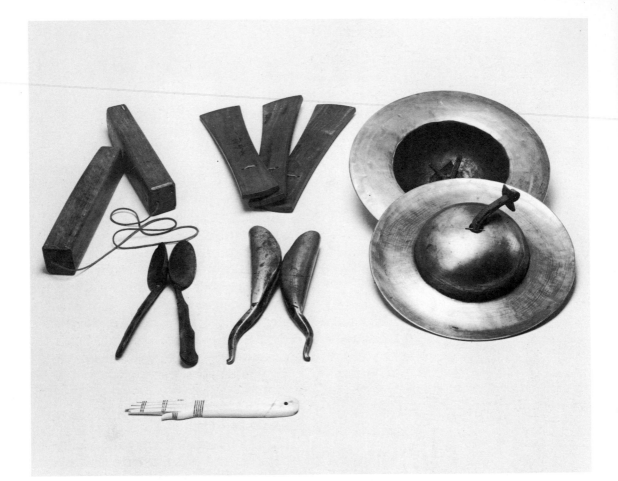

92 Concussion idiophones. Clockwise: hand-shaped ivory clapper, Egypt, about 1400 B.C., 1952.184; wooden spoons, Turkey, 1980.353,A; concussion sticks, Japan, 1911.232.25,A; rosewood triple clappers, China, 1887.191; cymbals, China, 1907.388,A; bronze concussion idiophones, Java, 1980.233-234.

More complex are the bar idiophones which, while they may have only one wooden bar fixed over a gourd resonator as in Malaysia, are much more frequently found as tuned bars. One of the earliest examples is the lithophone (a tuned series of stone bars) of China and Vietnam, which dates from neolithic times. A more familiar bar idiophone is the xylophone, a series of wooden bars placed over a series of graduated resonators. In Africa one resonator is attached beneath each bar **93**. In northern Ghana and the Ivory Coast xylophone ensembles are used at funerals, but they also perform with other stringed instruments such as the *kora* or small lutes to welcome important people, for feasts and to accompany dances. These bar idiophones, whether of stone, wood or metal, are melodic/rhythm instruments, for each bar is carefully tuned. Bar idiophones reached their highest development in Indonesia, particularly in Java and Bali, where several, with bars of wood and metal and sometimes

93 Senufo xylophonist playing at a funeral ceremony, Ivory Coast.   71

bamboo, and often placed over a cradle resonator, are combined with groups of gongs and gong chimes to form the famous *gamelan* orchestras of courts and temples **94**. Xylophones, like split-stringed zithers, were brought to Africa from Indonesia at least a thousand years ago. Today they are one of the most important and highly-regarded musical instruments of Africa.

94 Xylophone and beater from a nineteen-piece miniature gamelan orchestra modelled after the Sultan of Java's "band", U.C. 68.6,A.

95 Bronze gongs and chimes. Left to right: gong with central boss, Japan, 1910.74.3,A; struck temple bell, Japan, 1911.232.7; five tuned chimes and beater, Burma, 1865.64.24 & A-B & 25, 1903.391-392.

Gongs and bells are another major group of struck idiophones. Gongs are always round, always of metal (usually bronze), and it is the centre which vibrates and thus produces the maximum sound. Some are flat, some have bent-back rims, some have a central boss **95**. The so-called bronze 'drum' from the Shan States of Burma is a flat gong set horizontally on a deep circular bronze base-frame. The drums of the Trinidad steel bands, which are made from petrol containers, also belong to the gong family. Bells are usually made of metal in the Far East but in Africa are often of wood. They are struck on the rim rather than the centre, and the forms vary considerably. They may be struck internally with one clapper **96**, **97**, or externally with a beater **96**. They may be suspended in tuned sets called chimes as in this bronze set from Burma **95**, or as in the stone chimes of ancient China, many of which have recently been excavated. Bells may be suspended, held in the hand, worn around the neck of an animal, or rest on a stand **96**. Aside from their utilitarian value as animal bells, most bells have a ritual function. This is true of the Buddhist temple bells of the Far East and of those of the Hindus of India and Bali, and also applies to bells attached to shamans' drums of Siberia and Africa.

96 Bells. Left to right: two hand bells used in temple ceremonies, and a small bell for animals, Tibet, 1907.387, 1894.237, 1924.60; hanging temple bell, Burma, 1956.625; bullock bell in frame, Burma, 1955.80; hanging bell and beater, Japan, 1892.623,A; resting bell on stand, with beater, Japan, 595.31.C1-3.

97 African bells. Clockwise from left: bronze bell, southern Nigeria, 1906.551; wooden bell-shaped slit-drum, Cross River area, Nigeria, 1946.965; bronze bell, Benin, Nigeria, 1947.57; two Congolese wooden double bells with multiple clappers, 1902.312,213.

98 Slit-drums. Left to right: stylized wooden fish used in Buddhist temple ceremonies, Japan, 1911.232.31; small modern fish, Peking, China, 1980.457; large fish with a lemon in its mouth, *moku-gyo,* struck during temple services, Japan, 1910.74.1,A.

Finally, slit-drums, which are hollowed-out logs or pieces of bamboo, beaten on the edges of the slit, are an important group of struck idiophones. They are found in America, in Oceania, in Africa and in Asia, and within each continent there may be enormous variations in size. The Naga people of Assam have drums so large that a special house must be constructed for them. The slit-drum may be as much as thirteen metres long and has a ritual function. Much smaller slit-drums, from Pre-Columbian Mexico to the modern Far East, retain this role. One specialized form of slit-drum is that of the wooden 'fish'. Known in China for well over 2,000 years and used in temple services, early forms showed a naturalistic fish with a piece of fruit in its mouth; the *mokugyo* of Japan **98** retains this archaic design. The more recent shape has the fish bent backwards with its tail in its mouth, and very modern ones from Peking are even more stylized, and are painted in gold on the favourite colour, red **98**. Far Eastern slit-drums are not only used in temples today; small ones made of bamboo are struck by night-watchmen

99 Slit-drums. Left to right: Bali, 1980.235,A; Yombe people, Zaire, 1966.407,A; Congo region, 1901.357.

making their rounds, while in Bali they are used as signalling instruments **99**, and as scrapers (scraped idiophones or rasps). In Africa many anthropormorphic slit-drums, with human or animal heads, are found **99**, and while some small ones are repeatedly struck in a rhythmic pattern **99**, many are large and the different notes obtainable from the two sides of the slit make it possible to transmit messages in drum language when the local language is tonal. The West African slit-drum may also be part of an ensemble of various types of drums, adding a sharp note to the dance rhythms.

100 Rattle and clapper, Northwest Coast Indians of Canada. Top: rattle in the form of a raven, L.304.97. Bottom: clapper in the form of a killer-whale, 1951.223.

Another major group of idiophones is shaken, for example, rattles and jingles, sistra, pellet bells, and the *angklung* from Java. Rattles are hollow containers–seed pods, gourds, baskets, boxes, tubes or balls–which hold pellets. The appearance of rattles may differ. Northwest Coast Indians of Canada, for example, carve them with birds and animals **100**. For the shaman the instrument is used as a way of coming into contact with supernatural forces.

101 Mende woman with gourd rattle, Sierra Leone. 77

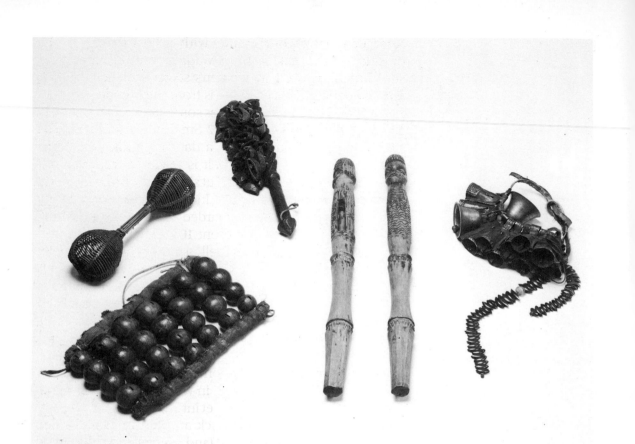

102 African rattles. Left to right: dance rattle, South Africa, 1894.366; double basketry rattle, Zaire, L.183.249; nut shell rattle with handle, Congo region, 1950.286; stick rattles, Yoruba people, Nigeria, 1931.94-95; dance girdle of nut shells and brass bells, Zaire, L.183.257.

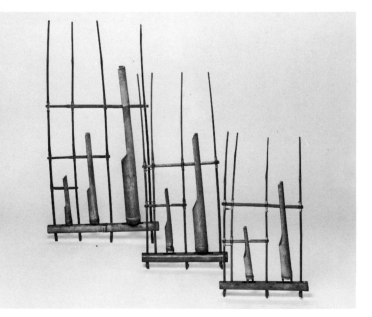

103 Sliding rattles, *angklung,* Java, 1896.309, 1936.329, 1933.255.

Another type of gourd rattle, with pellets strung on the outside of the calabash (nowadays buttons are often substituted), is used by women's secret societies for their masked dances. This example is from the Mende people of Sierra Leone **101**. Basketry rattles sometimes replace gourds, although the sound is softer **102**. Small gourd rattles may be strung together and worn as a dancing girdle **102**, while another variety of dancing belt is made by stringing nut shells and bells together **102**. Nut shells can also be fixed to a stick to make a hand rattle **102**. In contrast, the Yoruba stick rattles are staffs of power, guarded by soldiers, indicating that the *owa*, or ruler, is present **102**. Another specialized form of rattle is the pellet bell, a hollow piece of metal enclosing a pellet. Pellet bells are found wherever there is metalworking. A selection of bronze pellet bells from Japan **105** gives some idea of the possible shapes. The censer from the Ethiopian Christian Orthodox Church dispenses its incense to the tinkling sound of the pellet bells **105**.

One type of shaken idiophone appears to be peculiar to Java. This is the *angklung* **103**, in which pieces of bamboo, carefully tuned in octaves, are set into a groove in the base of a bamboo frame and slide back and forth when shaken. Each instrument has one note (and octave) and polyphonic music (several notes played simultaneously) is produced when several are combined in a group. Like most music played by bamboo instruments, the tone is delicate.

A final form of shaken idiophone is the sistrum, which consists of a number of discs or rings threaded onto a rod or

104 Sistra. Top: calabash sistrum, northern Nigeria, 1924.949. Bottom: top of a pilgrim's staff, Japan, 1911.232.17; Egyptian sistrum, about 1550 B.C., 1959.181; church sistrum, Ethiopia, 1980.383.

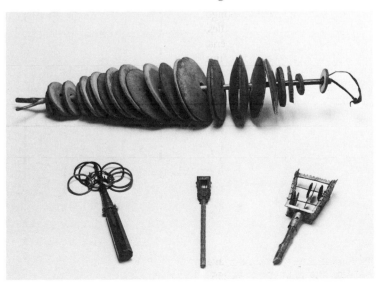

105 Pellet bells. Left to right: three bronze pellet bells, Japan, 1911.232.12,13,15; rattle of bronze pellet bells, Japan, 1911.232.9; church censer with pellet bells, Ethiopia, L.367.17.

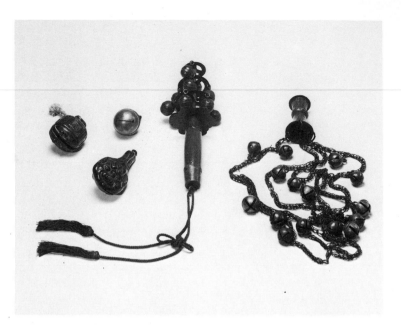

ring. The discs clash together when shaken. An instrument of the ancient world, it was known in Western Asia, in Egypt, and in Greece and Rome. The sistrum evidently travelled from Egypt to Ethiopia **104**. It is used today by all the congregation of the Ethiopian Christian Orthodox Church, where the only other instruments are the great drums struck by the dancing priests. A somewhat different form of sistrum, but also with religious connotations, is that used on the top of the staff of a Shintoist priest or pilgrim **104**. A West African sistrum, however, presents a total contrast, for the discs are made of calabash, and the instrument is used to accompany a flute or other single reed instrument of the Hausa or Fulani, and often beats the rhythm for a dance **104**.

Plucked idiophones are sounded by the bending and release of a flexible tongue, and only two types of instruments come into this category: mouth harps–which have been discussed under wind instruments, as they are a compound aerophone/idiophone–and the *sansa*, the pleasant-toned intimate instrument of Africa south of the Sahara **106, 107**. The soundbox of a *sansa* is formed of wood, gourd, or tortoise shell, and the tongues are made either of bamboo or iron. The iron may be locally smelted, but more frequently umbrella or bicycle wheel spokes are hammered flat to make the tongues. Young men walk along playing love songs on this easily made, easily carried, soft-voiced instrument.

106 Man playing a *sansa,* Sierra Leone.

107 *Sansas.* Back row: Cross River area, Nigeria, 1928.135; Zaire, 1909.466; Bonny, southern Nigeria, 716.100. Front row: Zaire, L.183.58; Malawi, 1931.390; Tanzania, 1950.79; Birom people, Jos, Nigeria, 1980.252; Congo region, 1907.305.

108   Friction idiophone in the form
      of a pig, New Ireland, 1948.364.

A small number of idiophones are sounded by friction. The rubbed wood friction idiophone from New Ireland **108** is a rare and highly developed instrument, which is cut into four sections and produces four notes when rubbed with a moistened hand; it is used in secret ceremonies and is called a *lounuet*.

Drums

Drums are the dominant rhythm instruments throughout the world. They are classified as membranophones because, to be a drum, an instrument must have a skin stretched over the opening of a body or a frame. Drums have as their primary function the providing of rhythm for music, dance and ceremonies. In this respect they are unlike idiophones, which may also be melodic instruments (such as xylophones, chimes, *sansas* or *angklung*) and whose function may be essentially concerned with magic (such as many rattles and slit-drums).

109 Detail of drummers from an 18th century Persian miniature painting (reproduced with the permission of the Trustees of the British Museum).

There are a great many possible ways of classifying the drums of the world: shape, material, function, number of membranes, method of fastening the skins, method of tuning, method of setting the membrane in motion, regional types, whether played singly or in ensembles–all are useful categories in one context or another.

Starting with the simplest classification, drums can have one or two membranes. Single membrane drums may be   83 very large–in West Africa drums over a metre in length are common **121**, and examples as long as three metres are known–or they may be tiny, such as the pottery *tarija* of Morocco, barely ten centimetres high **120**. The same degree of variety is found amongst the double membrane drums. Clearly, although this differentiation on the basis of membrane must be made, it is far too broad to be a useful indicator of what a drum looks or sounds like.

Shape is a more valuable method of classifying drums, because basically they fall into three main types: tubular drums, kettle-drums and frame drums.

110 Japanese drums. Left to right: waisted drum, 1911.232.1; double-sided frame drum, 1911.232.6; barrel-shaped drum, 1911.232.5.

Tubular drums vary considerably in size and appearance. They may be cylindrical **114**, barrel-shaped **110**, conical **115**, goblet-shaped **120**, waisted **110**, **112**, **114**, footed **114**, or handle drums **114**, **116**. Although most commonly made of wood, they can also be of gourd **114**, pottery **120**, or even of so unexpected a material as human skullcaps **112**. Some are elaborately carved **114**, or lacquered **110**, others hung with bells **114**, or ornamented with feathers **116**. Skins may be from goats, sheep or cattle. Snake or lizard skins are also used.

Many tubular drums shed fascinating side-lights on the societies which produce and play them. Choosing at random from the wealth of these drums, the master drummer's long drum of the Ashanti of Ghana **121** sets the rhythmic pattern for the drum ensemble. The music will vary for the different parts of a funeral, for marriage and

111 Sherpa monk using a waisted drum struck by pellets when twirled, northern Nepal.

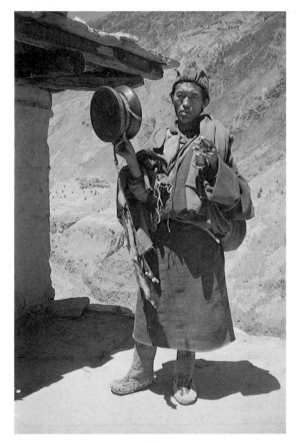

112 Pellet drum made of human skullcaps. Used in lamaist Buddhist temple ceremonies, Tibet, 1980.185.

113 Frame drum on stand, illustrated in a Chinese miniature painting.

114 African drums. Back row: conical drum, Cross River area, Nigeria, 399.1; footed drum, Yao people, Tanzania, 1900.9; carved drum, Baule people, Ivory Coast, 1939.137. Front row: waisted drum, Zambesi region, 1902.212; two pottery frame drums, Nigeria, 1980.118-119; gourd drum, Ghana, 1932.389; cylindrical drum, Malawi, 1894.53.

childbirth festivities; it will induce trance; certain rhythms accompany the prayers for rain and for a good harvest, while others help to ward off evil spirits. Within the Ashanti drum ensemble is another unusual drum: the talking drum. The two drumheads are attached to each other by lacings and the body of the drum is waisted. When held against the player's body his arm presses on the lacings and thus tightens and loosens the drumheads producing high, medium or low notes. Since the Ashanti language is a tonal one, the drum can reproduce the tonal pattern of a word. A selected vocabulary is used in drum language, and this is how the 'bush telegraph' works.

Other waisted drums are found on the other side of the world, and there seems to be no connection between them. For over a thousand years the musicians of Japan have used them as part of the Bugaku orchestra which leads the archaic style dances, and accompanies the Nō plays. There are at least a dozen waisted drums, each with its own name, its own style of decoration, its own playing position and its own definite role in court music **110**.

Another remarkable waisted drum is used in Tibet and also by lamaist Buddhists of Nepal and Mongolia. The

115 Long drums. Left to right: *darabuka,* Marsh Arabs, Iraq, 1980.315; double-membrane drum with beaters, used to call the spirits, Karo Batak people, Sumatra, 1980.243,A,B.

116 Drums from Papua New Guinea. Left to right: *warup,* Torres Straits, 1885.84; Trobriand Islands, 1883.91.5,3.

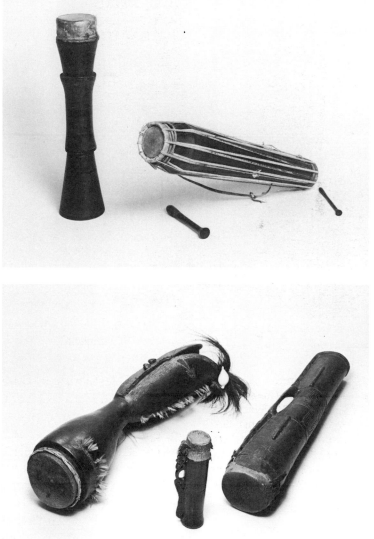

skullcap drum is most frequently used, but wooden skewomorphs (one material imitating another) are common. This drum is not beaten with a stick or with the hand, but has pellets, each fixed to a cord and tied to the central cloth ring **112**. When the drum is twirled the pellets hit the skins with a sharp sound. In the lamaist liturgy, this drum indicates a change from one section to another. It is also used to mark the periods of devotion **111**.

Kettledrums have a body made from a pot or other vessel (which may be of copper or bronze, even wood or gourd). They are all single membrane drums (as the base of a pot is closed) and the diameter of the skin may often be greater than the height of the drum. Widely distributed wherever pottery is made, the most familiar type is the double *naqqara* **120** of the Arabic countries which is used in processional music together with long trumpets and shawms. These three instruments are frequently depicted on Persian, Turkish and Moghul miniatures. The drummers are mounted, beating a pair of kettledrums, one on each side of the saddle. The drums are of different sizes, and hence produce different notes.

Kettledrums in Islamic countries are not reserved for military music; they are often used in Sufi music, and occasionally in Arabic classical music. The Indian derivative is the combination of *tabla* and *baya*, and so highly developed is classical Indian drumming that music on this pair of instruments is often played by a virtuoso.

The third major group of drums is composed of frame drums. In general these do not have a body, but only a frame over which the skin is stretched. It may be nailed on (nails ward off the evil eye) **110**, or glued, or secured with pegs **114, 117**; it may have one or two heads **117**. The frame may have cymbals or rings added to it **109, 119**. It may be beaten with the fingers in Islamic countries, or it may be struck with a beater as in the huge monastery drums of Tibet **118**. The frame is generally of wood, but it may be the rim of a pot **114**. Although almost always round, square-frame drums are sometimes found in North and West Africa **119**.

Frame drums are frequently associated with religious ritual. Shamans in Siberia, Central Asia, and amongst the American Indians, may use the frame drum as their main, or sometimes only, means of making contact with the supernatural powers. Such drums **117** are never used for secular purposes, for the instrument as well as the shaman is imbued with supernatural power. The huge frame drums of the Tibetan and Mongolian lamaist ritual **117, 118** seem to be related to shamanistic drums. Their deep booming notes are as frightening as the clash of cymbals, the harsh sounds of shawms, conches and long trumpets. In the Islamic world too, the frame drum plays a part in Sufi music in places as far apart as Morocco, Turkey and Central Asia. It is the instrument which serves to induce trance, sometimes in conjunction with flutes, but more often alone. It has half a dozen names or more, *duf, tar, daira, def, bendir, ganga* to

117 Frame drums from Nepal. Those on the left, 1980.193,A, and right, 1980.183,A, may be used by lamaist Buddhist monks and by shamans. The drum in the centre, 1980.192, is used only by shamans.

118 Large frame drum used in lamaist Buddhist temple ceremonies, Sherpa people, northern Nepal.

119 Arab frame drums. Square *duf*, Algeria, 1980.268; *duf* with cymbals (tambourine type), Syria, 1980.311.

89

120 Pottery drums from Morocco. Left to right: đouble *naqqara*, 1980.297; *tarija*, 1980.302; *agoual*, 1980.301.

name but a few. It is played by women as well as men, for every religious experience.

A final type of membranophone is not beaten as drums are; it is sounded by the friction of a cord or stick going through the skin, which is twisted to produce a rubbing sound. Like the friction idiophone, in parts of Africa this is considered to have magical powers connected with fertility. Recently, however, it has become a toy, to be whirled around the head. In India amongst some castes, it is played together with gourd pipes to charm the cobras **66**, and as protection against them.

121 Akan drum ensemble, Ghana.

Selected Discology

The following, which are all obtainable in the United Kingdom, are recordings of music played on types of instruments that are represented in the collections of the Royal Scottish Museum.

Africa

Central Africa, Anthology of the music of the Aka Pygmies (3 discs) OCORA 558-526-28
Ethiopia (3 discs) Tangent Records:

Central Highlands	TGM 101
Desert Nomads	TGM 102
Eritrea	TGM 103

Gambia, Mandinka, Kora OCORA OCR 70
Nigeria, Music of Central Nigeria OCORA OCR 85
Sierra Leone: Musiques traditionnelles OCORA 558-549

The Americas

The American Indian (3 discs) Everest Records 3450-3
Los Pampas, Flutes et harpes indiennes Vogue 400620

The Arab World

Egypt, The Musicians of the Nile (2 vols) OCORA 558-514, 558-525
Music in the World of Islam (6 discs) Tangent Records:

The Human Voice	TGS 131
Lutes	TGS 132
Strings	TGS 133
Flutes and Trumpets	TGS 134
Reeds and Bagpipes	TGS 135
Drums and Rhythm	TGS 136

Asia

Inde: Rajasthan OCORA OCR 81
Iran, Anthology of Traditional Music (2 discs) OCORA:

Tala'i	558-540
Kiani	558-550

Tibetan popular music and theatre OCORA OCR 62
Turkey, Turkish traditional music OCORA 558-584

Oceania

Indonesia, Traditional Music and Songs OCORA 558-502
Musique Mélanésienne 'Are 'Are (3 vols) Vogue 530104
Polyphonies des Îles Salomon Chant du Monde LDX 74663
Songs of Aboriginal Australia and Torres Straits Ethnic
   Folkways FE 4102

Publishers

Tangent Records	50 Stroud Green Road London N4 3EF
OCORA	Radio France Avenue President Kennedy 75016 Paris France
Chant du Monde and French Vogue	Musée de l'Homme Palais de Chaillot 75016 Paris France
Folkway Records	165 West 46th Street New York City USA
Everest Records	10920 Wilshire Blvd Los Angeles California USA

Selected Bibliography

The literature on music and musical instruments is immense. The following brief selection relates particularly to the types of instruments in the collections of the Royal Scottish Museum. Many of the titles include extensive bibliographies.

General

Blades, J, *Percussion Instruments and their History,* London, 1970

Dournon, G, *Guide for the Collection of Traditional Musical Instruments,* Paris, 1981

Ethnomusicology, Ann Arbor, Mich., I–; 1953–

Grove's Dictionary of Music and Musicians, 6th ed., London, 1980

Jenkins, J, *Ethnic Musical Instruments,* London, 1970
       –*International Directory of Musical Instrument Collections,* Büren, Netherlands, 1977

Journal of the International Folk Music Council, Columbia, NY., I–; 1949–

Merriam, A P, *Anthropology of Music,* Evanston, Ill., 1964

Sachs, C, *The History of Musical Instruments,* New York, 1940

Africa

African Music, Grahamstown, South Africa, I–; 1948–

Atkins, G, ed., *Manding Art and Civilisation,* London, 1972

Ames, D W, and King, A V, *Glossary of Hausa Music and its Social Contexts,* Evanston, Ill., 1971

Bebey, P, *African Music,* London, 1975

Berliner, P, *The Soul of Mbira: Music and Traditions of the Shona People of Zimbabwe,* Berkeley, Cal., 1979

Jones, A M, *Studies in African Music,* London, 1959

King, A, *Yoruba Sacred Music,* Ibadan, 1961

Kirby, P R, *The Musical Instruments of the Native Races of South Africa,* London, 1934, 2nd ed. 1965

Nketia, J, *African Music in Ghana,* Evanston, Ill., 1963
       –*The Music of Africa,* New York, 1974

Rycroft, D, *Zulu, Swazi and Xhosa Instrumental and Vocal Music,* Tervuren, 1969 (with sound disc, speed 33⅓ rpm)

Senoga-Zake, G, *Music of Kenya,* Nairobi, 1975

Wachsmann, K, ed., *Essays on Music and History in Africa,* Evanston, Ill., 1971

The Americas

Densmore, F, *Chippewa Music,* Bulletin of the Bureau of American Ethnology, Washington DC., 45, 1910
—*Mandan and Hidatsa Music,* ibid, 80, 1923
—*Music of the Indians of British Columbia,* ibid, 136(27), 1943
—*Technique in the music of the American Indians,* ibid, 151(36), 1953

Izikowitz, K, *Musical and other Sound Instruments of South American Indians,* Gothenburg, 1935

Stevenson, R, *Music in Aztec and Inca Territories,* Berkeley, Cal., 1968

The Arab World

d'Erlanger, R, *La musique arabe,* Paris, 6 Vols, 1930-1959

Jenkins, J, and Rovsing Olsen, P, *Music and Musical Instruments in the World of Islam,* London, 1976

Manniche, L, *Ancient Egyptian Musical Instruments,* Munich, 1975

Asia

Asian Music, New York, I–; 1968–

Belayev, U, *Central Asian Music,* Middletown, Conn., 1975

Emsheimer, E, *Music of the Mongols,* Stockholm, 1943

Fox-Strangways, A, *Music of Hindostan,* Oxford, 1914

Garfias, R, *Music of a Thousand Autumns,* Berkeley, Cal., 1975

Kunst, J, *Music in Java,* The Hague, 1949

Malm, W, *Japanese Music and Musical Instruments,* Rutland, Ver., 1959

McPhee, C, *Music in Bali,* New Haven, Conn., 1966

Morton, D, *The Traditional Instrumental Music of Thailand,* Los Angeles, Cal., 1976

National Academy of Arts, *Survey of Korean Arts: The Traditional Music,* Seoul, 1973

Picken, L, *Folk Musical Instruments of Turkey,* London, 1975

Slobin, M, *Music in the Culture of Northern Afghanistan,* Tucson, Ariz., 1976

Trân Văn Khê, *Viet-Nam,* Paris, 1967

Waley, A, *The Nō Plays of Japan,* London, 1921

de Zoete, B, and Spies, W, *Dance and Drama in Bali,* London, 1938, 2nd ed. 1958

Zonis, E, *Classical Persian Music, an Introduction,* Cambridge, Mass., 1973

Oceania

Andersen, J, *Maori Music with its Polynesian Background,* New Plymouth, NZ, 1934

Chenoweth, V, ed., *Musical Instruments of Papua New Guinea,* Papua New Guinea, 1972

Ellis, C, *Aboriginal Music Making: Central Australian Music,* Adelaide, 1964

Kunst, J, *Music in New Guinea,* The Hague, 1967